MathFlare

Name: _______________________

Class: __________

Teacher: _______________________

Introduction

As parents and educators, we recognize the pivotal role mathematics plays in shaping a child's academic journey and future success. Yet, the path to mathematical proficiency can often seem daunting, fraught with challenges and complexities. That's where the transformative power of MathFlare Workbooks shine through, illuminating the way forward with clarity, precision, and purpose.

Introducing MathFlare Workbooks – a beacon of guidance, a testament to excellence, and a catalyst for achievement. Crafted with meticulous care and expertise, MathFlare Workbooks stand as paragons of educational excellence, designed to nurture young minds, ignite a passion for learning, and develop a deep-rooted understanding of mathematical concepts.

Picture this: your child eagerly delves into the pages of Mathflare Workbook, greeted by a step-by-step guide illuminated with vivid examples that demystify complex mathematical concepts. With each turn of the page, they embark on a journey of discovery, encountering thoughtfully curated practice questions that reinforce learning and hone problem-solving skills. And when they unveil the answers to those very questions, a sense of accomplishment blossoms within them – a tangible reward for their hard work and dedication.

But MathFlare Workbooks are more than just tools for learning; they are pathways to comprehension, fostering a deep-seated understanding of mathematical concepts through a sequential, logical flow. From fundamental principles to advanced problem-solving strategies, every chapter builds upon the last, ensuring a robust foundation upon which future knowledge can be constructed.

As parents, we yearn for nothing more than to see our children thrive, to witness the spark of inspiration ignited within them as they conquer academic challenges with confidence and poise. MathFlare Workbooks serve as partners in this noble endeavor, offering not just practice questions, but the keys to unlocking a world of opportunity.

And for teachers, MathFlare Workbooks stand as invaluable allies in the quest to cultivate mathematical proficiency in the classroom. With answers readily available, instructors can focus on guiding and nurturing their students, confident in the knowledge that MathFlare Workbooks provide a solid framework upon which to build.

In the pages of MathFlare Workbooks, we find not just the promise of academic excellence, but the seeds of a brighter tomorrow. So let us embrace the power of mathematics, let us champion the journey of learning, and let us pave the way for a generation of young minds poised to shape the world. With MathFlare Workbooks as our guide, the possibilities are infinite, and the future, bright.

Table of Contents

MathFlare
MATH
WORKBOOK
Grade 2
Step by Step Guide
and Essential Practice
with Answers
Addition Subtraction
Multiplication
Place Value and Expanded Notations
Geometry
MathFlare Publishing

MathFlare
MATH
WORKBOOK
Grade 2-3
Step by Step Guide
and Essential Practice
with Answers
Addition Subtraction
Multiplication and Division
Place Value and Expanded Notations
Geometry
MathFlare Publishing

MathFlare
MATH
WORKBOOK
Grade 3
Step by Step Guide
and Essential Practice
with Answers
Multiplication and Division
Decimals
Place Value and Expanded Notations
Fractions and Geometry
MathFlare Publishing

MathFlare
MATH
WORKBOOK
Grade 1
Step by Step Guide
and Essential Practice
with Answers
Counting and Numbers
Addition and Subtraction
Understanding Time
MathFlare Publishing

MathFlare
MATH
WORKBOOK
Grade 1-2
Step by Step Guide
and Essential Practice
with Answers
Counting and Numbers
Addition and Subtraction
Understanding Time
MathFlare Publishing

MathFlare
MATH
WORKBOOK
Grade 3-4
Step by Step Guide
and Essential Practice
with Answers
Addition Subtraction
Multiplication Division
Place Value and Expanded Notations
Fractions and Geometry
MathFlare Publishing

MathFlare
MATH
WORKBOOK
Grade 4
Step by Step Guide
and Essential Practice
with Answers
Addition Subtraction
Multiplication Division
Place Value and Expanded Notations
Fractions and Geometry
MathFlare Publishing

MathFlare
MATH
WORKBOOK
Grade 4-5
Step by Step Guide
and Essential Practice
with Answers
Multiplication Division
Place Value and Expanded Notations
Fractions and Geometry
Unit Conversion
MathFlare Publishing

MathFlare
MATH
WORKBOOK
5
Step by Step Guide
and Essential Practice
with Answers
Multiplication Division
Place Value and Expanded Notations
Fractions and Geometry
Unit Conversion
MathFlare Publishing

MathFlare
MATH
WORKBOOK
5-6
Step by Step Guide
and Essential Practice
with Answers
Multiplication Division
Place Value and Expanded Notations
Fractions and Geometry
Units and Statistics
MathFlare Publishing

MathFlare
MATH
WORKBOOK
6
Step by Step Guide
and Essential Practice
with Answers
Integers and Statistics
Arithmetic and Pre-Algebra
Fractions and Geometry
Ratio and Percentage
MathFlare Publishing

MathFlare
MATH
WORKBOOK
6-7
Step by Step Guide
and Essential Practice
with Answers
Arithmetic and Pre-Algebra
Ratio, Percent Proportion
Geometry
Statistics
MathFlare Publishing

MathFlare
MATH
WORKBOOK
7
Step by Step Guide
and Essential Practice
with Answers
Pre-Algebra
Ratio, Percent Proportion
Geometry
Statistics
MathFlare Publishing

MathFlare
MATH
WORKBOOK
7-8
Step by Step Guide
and Essential Practice
with Answers
Pre-Algebra
Ratio, Percent Proportion
Geometry and Cartesian Plane
Statistics
MathFlare Publishing

MathFlare
MATH
WORKBOOK
8-9
Step by Step Guide
and Essential Practice
with Answers
Pre-Algebra
Ratio, Proportion and Percentage
Linear Equations
Geometry and Cartesian Plane
MathFlare Publishing

MathFlare
MATH
WORKBOOK
8
Step by Step Guide
and Essential Practice
with Answers
Pre-Algebra
Percentage
Linear Equations
Geometry
MathFlare Publishing

Counting and Numbers

Counting Up:

Counting the numbers in ascending order or adding numbers in a sequence.

168	169	170	171	172	173	174	175	176	177

Counting Down:

Counting the numbers in descending order or subtracting numbers in a sequence.

249	248	247	246	245	244	243	242	241	240

Counting Patterns:

It refers to sequences of numbers that follow a specific rule or pattern: such as counting by 2s and 3s, adding 2s and 3s in sequence.

Count by 2s

Count by 2 from 312 to 330

312	314	316	318	320	322	324	326	328	330

Compare the Numbers:

We use signs to compare the numbers. Such as, > = greater than, < = less than, and = equal to.

For Instance: if we compare, 754 and 51, we can write:

$$754 > 51$$

This means that 754 is greater than 51. In other words, 754 is a larger number than 51.

Circle the Numbers:

In this lesson, we try to understand and recognize the numbers. The task is to identify the numbers that are smallest, largest, odd or even. For instance, we have circled the smallest and largest numbers in the following numbers.

948, 69, 529, 523, 82

948 is the largest number and 69 is the smallest number.

Missing Numbers:

In this exercise, one or two numbers are given, and the task is to find the numbers that come before, between and after those numbers. For example:

296 *297* 298 , *472* 473

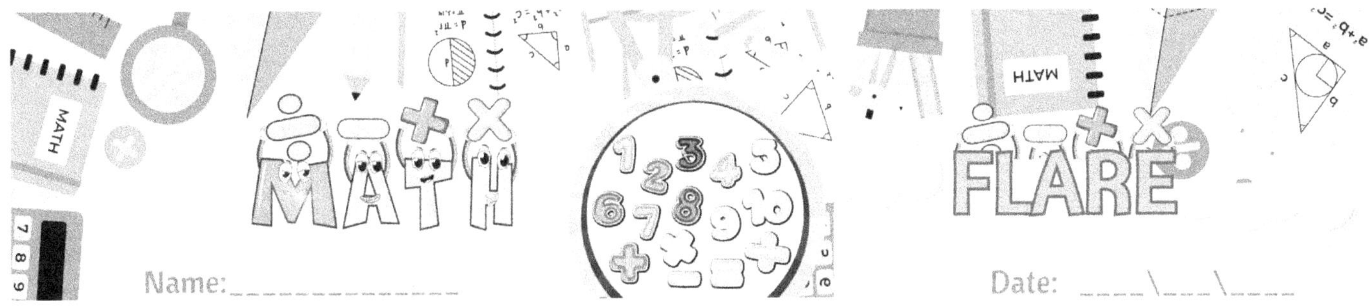

Counting Up

Fill in the missing numbers by counting up.

1. | | | 259 | | | 255 | | | |
| --- | --- | --- | --- | --- | --- | --- | --- | --- |
| | | | | | | | | |

2. | | | | 730 | 728 | | | | |
| --- | --- | --- | --- | --- | --- | --- | --- | --- |
| | | | | | | | | |

3. | 257 | | | | | | | | 249 |
| --- | --- | --- | --- | --- | --- | --- | --- | --- |
| | | | | | | | | |

4. | | | | | | | | 608 | 607 |
| --- | --- | --- | --- | --- | --- | --- | --- | --- |
| | | | | | | | | |

5. | | | | 633 | | | | | 628 |
| --- | --- | --- | --- | --- | --- | --- | --- | --- |
| | | | | | | | | |

6. | 186 | | 184 | | | | | | |
| --- | --- | --- | --- | --- | --- | --- | --- | --- |
| | | | | | | | | |

7.

	763								755

8.

	93						87		

9.

				718			715	

10.

	272				268			

11.

	387			383			

12.

	254	253						

13.

48					43			

14.

				445			442		

15.

							32	30

16.

854				849			

17.

			314				309

18.

465		462					

19.

11				6			

20.

		157			153		

21.

		311							304

22.

	148	147							

23.

293						287			

24.

			621	620					

25.

	871		869						

26.

	667		665						

27.

						295		292	

28.

678				673				

29.

							878	876

30.

	355				350			

31.

43								34

32.

					534		531

33.

	411					405	

34.

222				216		

35.

					49		46	

36.

	577			573				

37.

31			27					

38.

					590		588	

39.

			38	36				

40.

				15		13		

41.

	51			47				

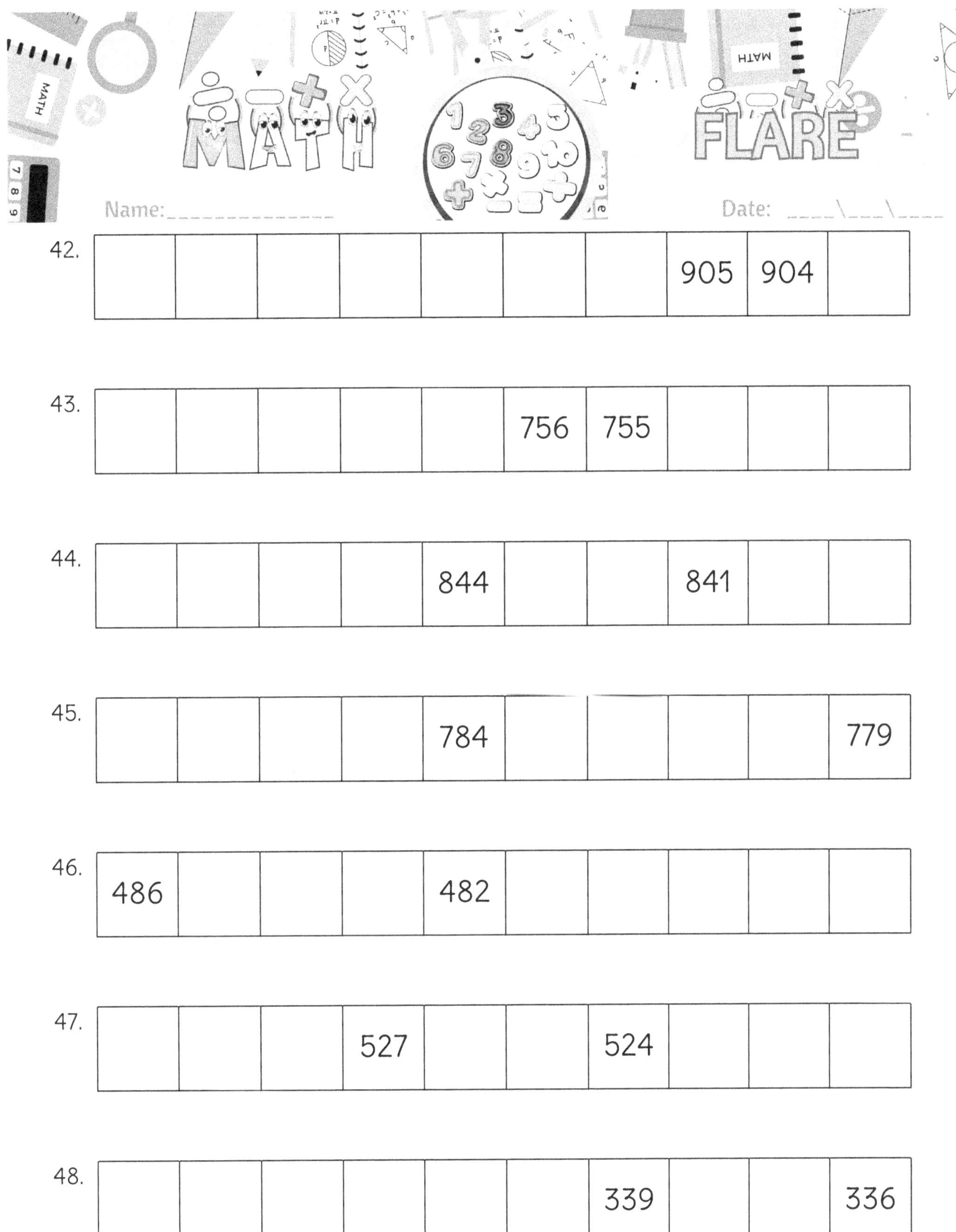

42.

							905	904	

43.

					756	755			

44.

				844			841		

45.

				784					779

46.

486				482					

47.

			527			524			

48.

						339			336

Name:_______________   Date: ____________

Counting Down
Fill in the missing numbers by counting Down.

49.

	17	16						

50.

267	266							

51.

				168	167			

52.

						320	319	

53.

					56	55		

54.

				919	918			

55.

			701	700					

56.

				336	335				

57.

	806	805							

58.

					703	702			

59.

						429	428		

60.

504	503								

61.

	777	776							

62.

537	536							

63.

						356	355	

64.

		276	275					

65.

		707	706					

66.

	608	607						

67.

	421	420						

68.

						807	806	

69.

		515	514						

70.

				910	909				

71.

							728	727	

72.

718	717								

73.

					456	455			

74.

							250	249	

75.

					590	589			

76. | 500 | 499 | | | | | | | |

77. | | | | | | | | 249 | 248 | |

78. | | | | | 324 | 323 | | | | |

79. | | | | | | | 568 | 567 | | |

80. | | | | | | | | 387 | 386 | |

81. | | | | 319 | 318 | | | | | |

82. | | | | | 723 | 722 | | | | |

83. | 446 | 445 | | | | | | | | |
|---|---|---|---|---|---|---|---|---|---|

84. | | | | | | | | 197 | 196 | |
|---|---|---|---|---|---|---|---|---|---|

85. | | 123 | 122 | | | | | | | |
|---|---|---|---|---|---|---|---|---|---|

86. | | | | | | 184 | 183 | | | |
|---|---|---|---|---|---|---|---|---|---|

87. | 851 | 850 | | | | | | | | |
|---|---|---|---|---|---|---|---|---|---|

88. | | | | | 777 | 776 | | | | |
|---|---|---|---|---|---|---|---|---|---|

89. | | | | 800 | 799 | | | | | |
|---|---|---|---|---|---|---|---|---|---|

90. | | | 492 | 491 | | | | | | |
91. | | 757 | 756 | | | | | | | |
92. | | 896 | 895 | | | | | | | |
93. | | | 746 | 745 | | | | | | |
94. | | | | | 545 | 544 | | | | |
95. | | | 404 | 403 | | | | | | |
96. | | | | 13 | 12 | | | | | |

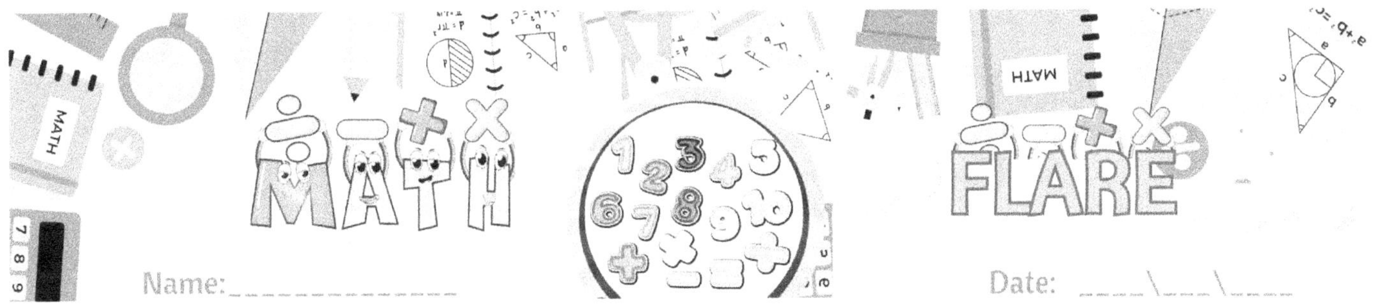

Name:____________________   Date: _______________

Counting Patterns

Complete the counting tables.

97. Count by 4 from 746 to 782

746									

98. Count by 4 from 837 to 873

								869	

99. Count by 3 from 194 to 221

		203							

100. Count by 4 from 786 to 822

		794							

101. Count by 4 from 32 to 68

| | | | 44 | | | | | | |

102. Count by 4 from 242 to 278

| | | | | | | | | | 278 |

103. Count by 2 from 34 to 52

| | | | | | | | 48 | | |

104. Count by 4 from 219 to 255

| | | | | | | | 247 | | |

105. Count by 3 from 461 to 488

| | | 467 | | | | | | | |

106. Count by 2 from 870 to 888

		874						

107. Count by 4 from 762 to 798

							794	

108. Count by 4 from 941 to 977

		949						

109. Count by 4 from 482 to 518

							510	

110. Count by 3 from 479 to 506

							500	

111. Count by 3 from 832 to 859

					847				

112. Count by 4 from 457 to 493

	461								

113. Count by 5 from 456 to 501

					481				

114. Count by 3 from 302 to 329

									329

115. Count by 4 from 687 to 723

687									

116. Count by 2 from 480 to 498

		484							

117. Count by 3 from 751 to 778

							775	

118. Count by 2 from 365 to 383

								383

119. Count by 3 from 765 to 792

				780				

120. Count by 3 from 418 to 445

	421							

121. Count by 3 from 982 to 1009

	985							

122. Count by 5 from 643 to 688

643								

123. Count by 4 from 736 to 772

		744						

124. Count by 3 from 846 to 873

846								

125. Count by 2 from 674 to 692

		678						

126. Count by 3 from 905 to 932

			914					

127. Count by 5 from 152 to 197

						182		

128. Count by 4 from 893 to 929

	897							

129. Count by 3 from 177 to 204

		183						

130. Count by 3 from 547 to 574

							571	

131. Count by 5 from 321 to 366

		331							

132. Count by 4 from 713 to 749

		721							

133. Count by 3 from 575 to 602

								599	

134. Count by 3 from 945 to 972

					960				

135. Count by 4 from 252 to 288

							280		

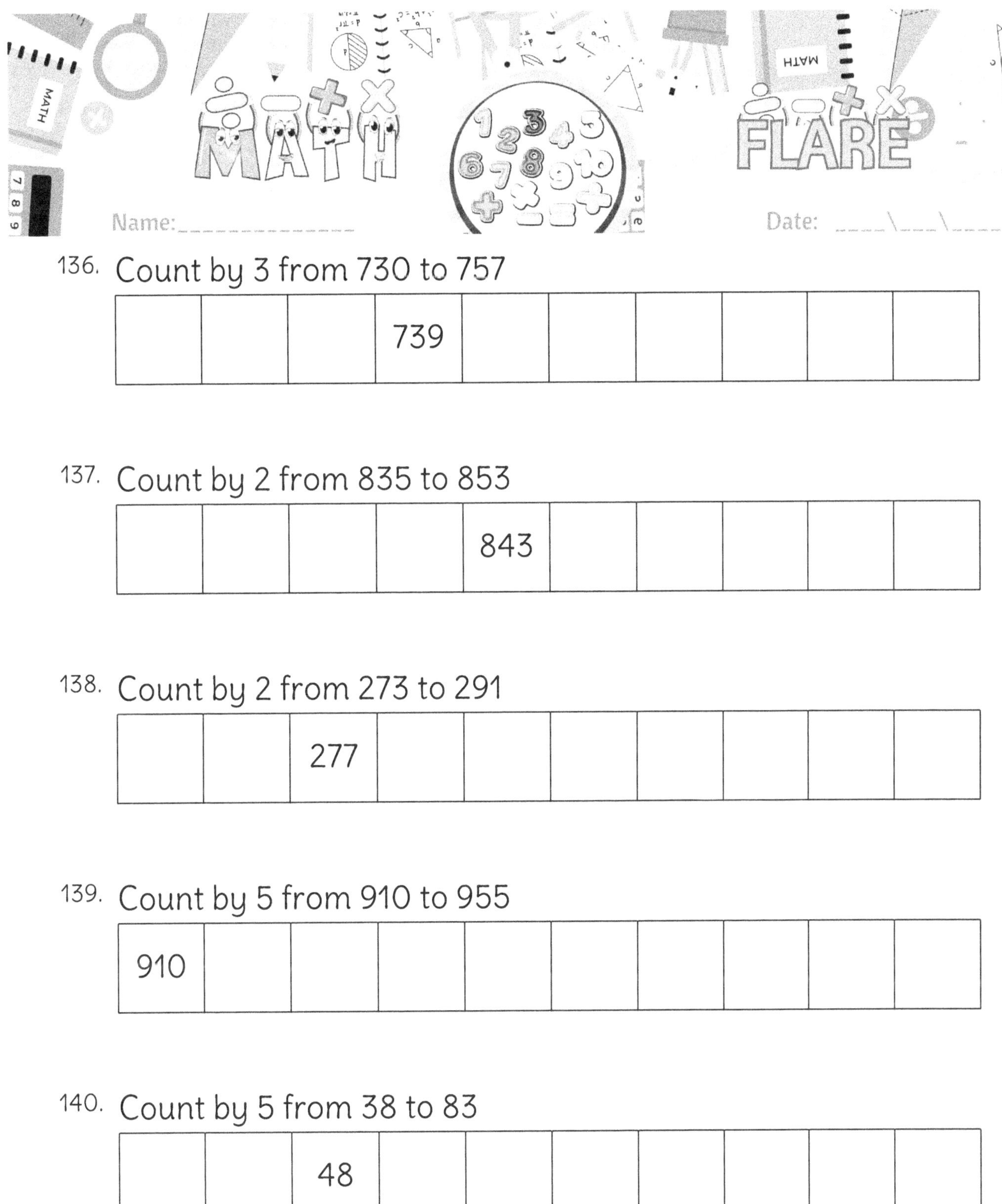

Name:____________________   Date: _______________

136. Count by 3 from 730 to 757

			739						

137. Count by 2 from 835 to 853

				843					

138. Count by 2 from 273 to 291

		277							

139. Count by 5 from 910 to 955

910									

140. Count by 5 from 38 to 83

		48							

141. Count by 2 from 401 to 419

									419

142. Count by 2 from 929 to 947

		935							

143. Count by 3 from 173 to 200

							194		

144. Count by 4 from 313 to 349

			333					

145. Count by 2 from 239 to 257

				249				

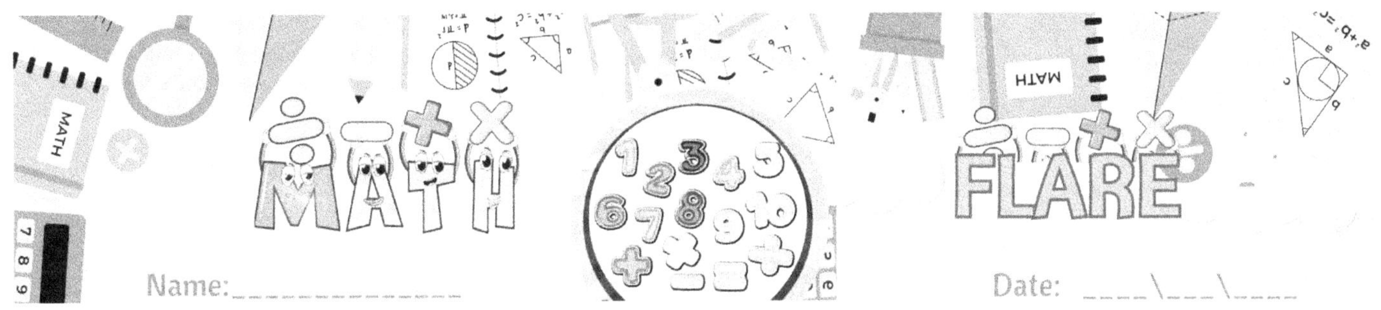

Name:________________   Date: ______________

Compare the Numbers

Add: > or < or = to make the following statements true.

146. 402 ____ 879

147. 66 ____ 157

148. 957 ____ 95

149. 195 ____ 196

150. 907 ____ 825

151. 649 ____ 992

152. 591 ____ 938

153. 543 ____ 390

154. 549 ____ 530

155. 637 ____ 503

156. 71 ____ 233

157. 622 ____ 54

158. 536 ____ 200

159. 333 ____ 498

160. 951 ___ 798

161. 263 ___ 919

162. 711 ___ 506

163. 709 ___ 310

164. 413 ___ 676

165. 121 ___ 203

166. 377 ___ 542

167. 984 ___ 283

168. 971 ___ 27

169. 519 ___ 148

170. 626 ___ 767

171. 354 ___ 569

172. 685 ___ 403

173. 886 ___ 170

174. 257 ___ 12

175. 620 ___ 757

176. 762 ____ 696

177. 244 ____ 110

178. 562 ____ 730

179. 282 ____ 85

180. 229 ____ 234

181. 977 ____ 872

182. 409 ____ 434

183. 126 ____ 529

184. 249 ____ 339

185. 82 ____ 510

186. 681 ____ 185

187. 872 ____ 185

188. 444 ____ 694

189. 234 ____ 308

190. 619 ____ 540

191. 53 ____ 401

Name:____________________   Date: ____________

192. 57 ____ 364

193. 440 ____ 680

194. 298 ____ 875

195. 720 ____ 241

196. 744 ____ 434

197. 919 ____ 393

198. 790 ____ 481

199. 160 ____ 252

200. 277 ____ 358

201. 921 ____ 918

202. 929 ____ 111

203. 77 ____ 578

204. 824 ____ 60

205. 665 ____ 867

206. 497 ____ 974

207. 465 ____ 688

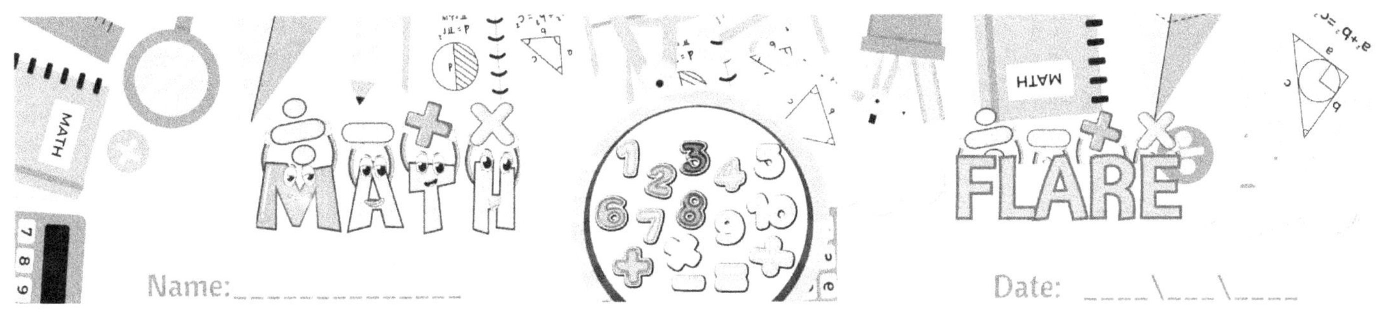

Circle the Numbers

Circle the smallest and biggest number in each group.

208. 553 277 76 484 404

209. 911 791 744 69 997

210. 211 724 271 301 581

211. 78 418 656 245 867

212. 169 512 873 103 74

213. 504 66 597 957 999

214. 687 302 390 250 904

215. 273 436 90 104 609

216. 439 83 697 164 954

217. 383 523 55 546 165

218. 717 728 289 126 182

219. 41 404 972 411 899

220. 846 194 787 69 310

221. 909 335 21 396 308

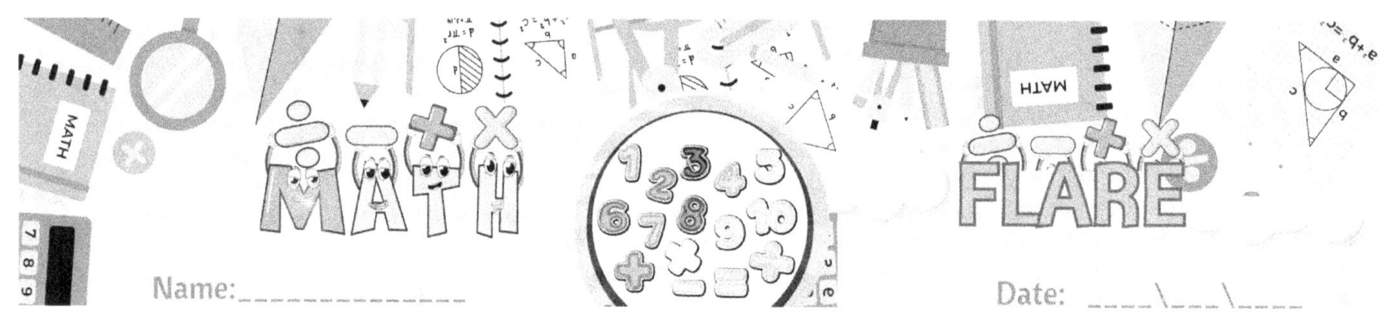

222. 641 328 552 636 428

223. 87 814 709 149 690

224. 980 11 52 792 283

225. 959 13 265 69 863

226. 869 464 679 204 763

227. 245 295 628 854 45

228. 49 503 659 239 524

229. 389 177 652 697 95

230. 227 694 824 720 919

231. 835 143 995 786 351

232. 896 71 951 532 438

233. 178 649 348 873 184

234. 791 187 855 105 642

235. 478 352 812 269 893

236. 783 361 568 973 637

237. 175 640 958 285 927

238. 103 300 842 503 148

239. 977 551 127 800 346

240. 740 828 778 513 304

241. 40 839 719 78 441

242. 484 330 726 892 568

243. 536 503 978 895 264

244. 538 690 63 946 82

245. 491 345 352 956 665

246. 926 226 13 922 154

247. 954 582 55 670 597

248. 336 920 881 844 444

249. 772 573 949 935 612

250. 475 573 232 536 808

251. 50 765 832 432 812

252. 695 487 763 413 514

253. 258 317 804 739 613

254. 953 448 308 298 928

255. 618 809 219 502 309

256. 917 395 417 345 190

257. 354 994 476 115 104

258. 190 749 622 857 902

259. 848 157 468 330 186

260. 455 769 210 323 658

261. 27 265 934 608 191

262. 241 546 331 123 895

263. 300 71 419 223 161

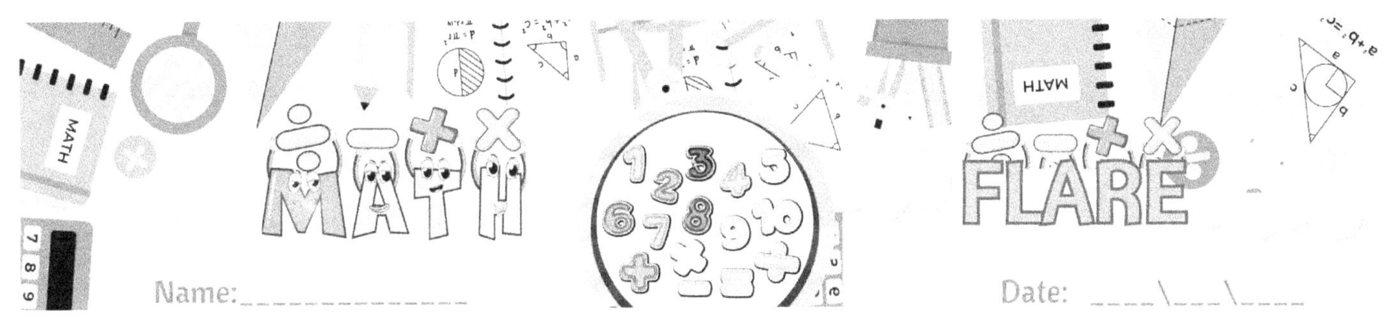

Name:_______________   Date: ____________

264. 264 840 690 636 423   265. 204 825 451 395 80

266. 461 341 889 316 854   267. 148 186 94 686 164

268. 89 61 868 923 863   269. 643 419 500 961 602

270. 777 738 246 170 922   271. 614 80 574 899 454

272. 201 813 539 528 729   273. 899 657 15 269 747

274. 115 977 733 59 72   275. 204 972 766 772 780

276. 784 326 490 793 302   277. 723 95 720 394 240

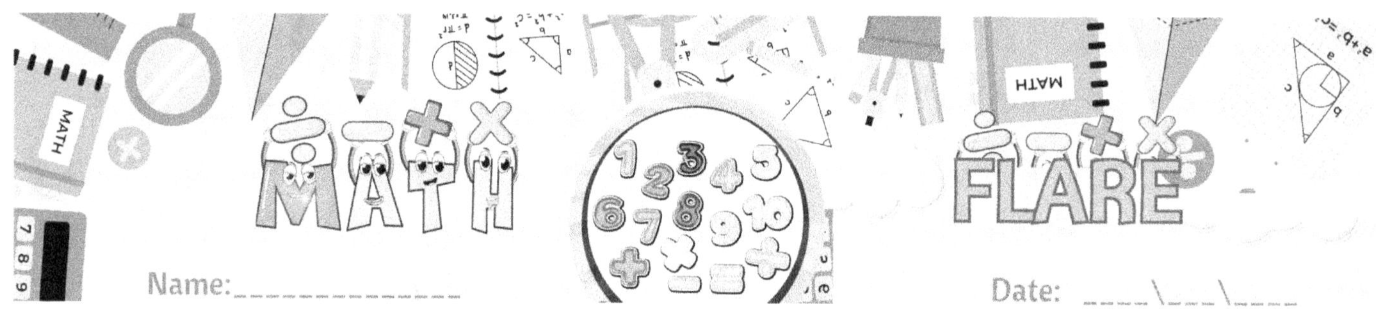

Missing Numbers

Fill in the missing numbers, before and after and between.

278. _____ 70 _____

279. 194 _____

280. _____ 963

281. _____ 522

282. 195 _____ 197

283. _____ 986

284. 231 _____

285. 488 _____ 490

286. 6 ___

287. _____ 99 _____

288. _____ 643

289. 801 _____

290. 670 _____ 672

291. _____ 325 _____

292. 226 _____

293. 804 _____ 806

MathFlare -Counting and Numbers 1st and 2nd Grade

34

294. 620 _______

295. _______ 680 _______

296. _______ 784 _______

297. 97 _______ 99

298. _______ 683 _______

299. 572 _______ 574

300. _______ 795

301. _______ 97

302. _______ 306 _______

303. 717 _______ 719

304. _______ 623 _______

305. 598 _______ 600

306. 811 _______

307. 562 _______

308. 951 _______ 953

309. 115 _______

310. 159 _______

311. 785 _______

312. 536 _______ 538

313. _______ 18 _______

314. _______ 92

315. 36 _______

316. 742 _______ 744

317. _______ 326

318. 779 _______

319. _______ 442 _______

320. 289 _______ 291

321. 315 _______ 317

322. 431 _______ 433

323. _______ 692 _______

324. 939 _______

325. 845 _______ 847

326. _______ 519

327. _______ 651 _______

328. 594 _______ 596

329. _______ 740

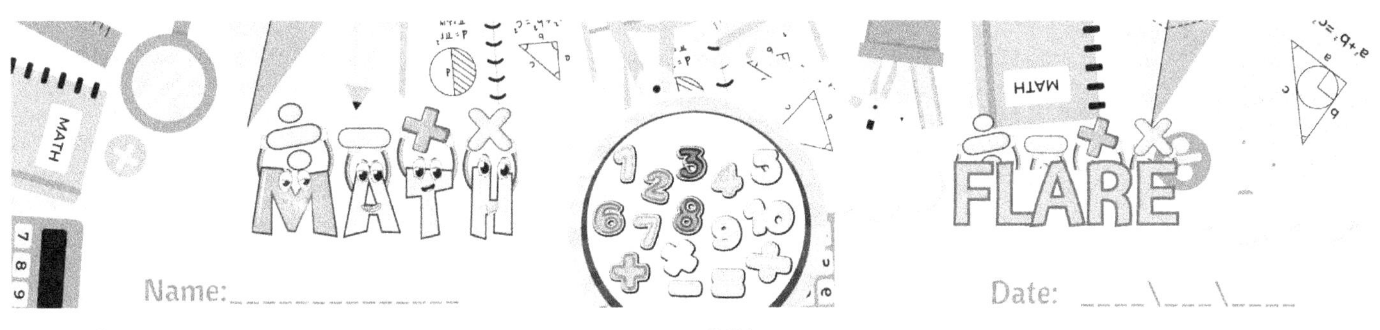

330. 485 ______

331. ______ 818

332. ______ 641 ______

333. 12 ______ 14

334. ______ 750

335. 309 ______ 311

336. ______ 336

337. ______ 899

338. 732 ______ 734

339. ______ 771 ______

340. ______ 295

341. 564 ______

342. 455 ______

343. ______ 493

344. ______ 343 ______

345. 697 ______ 699

346. 310 ______

347. 240 ______

Ordering Numbers

Order the numbers.

348.		349.		350.	
512	_____	468	_____	393	_____
430	_____	376	_____	953	_____
164	_____	520	_____	645	_____
479	_____	186	_____	587	_____

351.		352.		353.	
748	_____	341	_____	737	_____
602	_____	155	_____	841	_____
644	_____	117	_____	504	_____
339	_____	655	_____	342	_____

354.		355.		356.	
559	_____	421	_____	668	_____
856	_____	989	_____	167	_____
216	_____	522	_____	210	_____
595	_____	174	_____	444	_____

357.		358.		359.	
548	_____	544	_____	457	_____
506	_____	475	_____	412	_____
583	_____	636	_____	509	_____
361	_____	414	_____	123	_____

360.	626 ____ 871 ____ 277 ____ 588 ____	361.	536 ____ 836 ____ 149 ____ 607 ____	362.	758 ____ 179 ____ 569 ____ 191 ____	
363.	274 ____ 944 ____ 673 ____ 969 ____	364.	330 ____ 358 ____ 243 ____ 783 ____	365.	183 ____ 320 ____ 802 ____ 536 ____	
366.	108 ____ 580 ____ 498 ____ 297 ____	367.	796 ____ 889 ____ 622 ____ 134 ____	368.	712 ____ 456 ____ 975 ____ 763 ____	
369.	464 ____ 906 ____ 544 ____ 744 ____	370.	512 ____ 739 ____ 539 ____ 217 ____	371.	368 ____ 728 ____ 494 ____ 535 ____	

372.
316 _____
134 _____
613 _____
986 _____

373.
277 _____
681 _____
371 _____
571 _____

374.
385 _____
421 _____
638 _____
821 _____

375.
873 _____
382 _____
479 _____
984 _____

376.
277 _____
775 _____
157 _____
652 _____

377.
369 _____
141 _____
380 _____
651 _____

378.
168 _____
495 _____
187 _____
808 _____

379.
677 _____
843 _____
989 _____
275 _____

380.
782 _____
635 _____
973 _____
870 _____

381.
190 _____
200 _____
718 _____
923 _____

382.
985 _____
348 _____
509 _____
846 _____

383.
540 _____
976 _____
961 _____
877 _____

384. 236 ______
400 ______
719 ______
318 ______

385. 889 ______
334 ______
830 ______
888 ______

386. 130 ______
393 ______
304 ______
462 ______

387. 642 ______
802 ______
287 ______
153 ______

388. 268 ______
423 ______
457 ______
878 ______

389. 820 ______
985 ______
340 ______
759 ______

390. 701 ______
882 ______
212 ______
955 ______

391. 482 ______
915 ______
754 ______
166 ______

392. 856 ______
370 ______
829 ______
407 ______

393. 692 ______
143 ______
147 ______
940 ______

394. 738 ______
789 ______
907 ______
859 ______

395. 813 ______
943 ______
841 ______
952 ______

396.	904 ____	397.	248 ____	398.	726 ____
	993 ____		280 ____		148 ____
	171 ____		348 ____		220 ____
	497 ____		977 ____		444 ____

399.	898 ____	400.	776 ____	401.	911 ____
	593 ____		937 ____		974 ____
	149 ____		400 ____		353 ____
	236 ____		353 ____		904 ____

402.	538 ____	403.	862 ____	404.	511 ____
	174 ____		298 ____		794 ____
	802 ____		431 ____		170 ____
	182 ____		492 ____		515 ____

405.	690 ____	406.	319 ____	407.	966 ____
	668 ____		893 ____		693 ____
	563 ____		704 ____		817 ____
	697 ____		377 ____		743 ____

408.	274 ____	409.	652 ____	410.	699 ____
	927 ____		345 ____		261 ____
	443 ____		138 ____		657 ____
	405 ____		639 ____		643 ____
411.	982 ____	412.	342 ____	413.	644 ____
	867 ____		511 ____		469 ____
	885 ____		656 ____		524 ____
	574 ____		752 ____		875 ____
414.	269 ____	415.	584 ____	416.	444 ____
	481 ____		451 ____		629 ____
	688 ____		764 ____		923 ____
	488 ____		530 ____		397 ____
417.	157 ____	418.	199 ____	419.	762 ____
	336 ____		807 ____		371 ____
	161 ____		343 ____		691 ____
	215 ____		680 ____		954 ____

420. 282 _____
820 _____
263 _____
802 _____

421. 317 _____
573 _____
269 _____
323 _____

422. 630 _____
203 _____
454 _____
447 _____

423. 713 _____
588 _____
358 _____
298 _____

424. 408 _____
409 _____
650 _____
738 _____

425. 238 _____
107 _____
727 _____
656 _____

426. 759 _____
810 _____
189 _____
944 _____

427. 466 _____
220 _____
266 _____
335 _____

428. 166 _____
837 _____
536 _____
694 _____

429. 453 _____
895 _____
961 _____
147 _____

430. 112 _____
492 _____
660 _____
132 _____

431. 511 _____
612 _____
163 _____
769 _____

432. 566 _____
      541 _____
      667 _____
      465 _____

433. 393 _____
      365 _____
      503 _____
      195 _____

434. 467 _____
      192 _____
      962 _____
      810 _____

435. 570 _____
      872 _____
      956 _____
      743 _____

436. 342 _____
      146 _____
      679 _____
      482 _____

437. 366 _____
      249 _____
      156 _____
      169 _____

438. 853 _____
      157 _____
      497 _____
      255 _____

439. 624 _____
      270 _____
      171 _____
      822 _____

440. 187 _____
      492 _____
      865 _____
      801 _____

441. 920 _____
      529 _____
      849 _____
      791 _____

442. 638 _____
      656 _____
      420 _____
      761 _____

443. 520 _____
      862 _____
      284 _____
      265 _____

ANSWERS

Page 1:   Counting Up

1.

| 261 | 260 | **259** | 258 | 257 | 256 | **255** | 254 | 253 | 252 |

2.

| 733 | 732 | 731 | **730** | 729 | **728** | 727 | 726 | 725 | 724 |

3.

| 258 | **257** | 256 | 255 | 254 | 253 | 252 | 251 | 250 | **249** |

4.

| 616 | 615 | 614 | 613 | 612 | 611 | 610 | 609 | **608** | **607** |

5.

| 637 | 636 | 635 | 634 | **633** | 632 | 631 | 630 | 629 | **628** |

6.

| **186** | 185 | **184** | 183 | 182 | 181 | 180 | 179 | 178 | 177 |

7.

| 764 | **763** | 762 | 761 | 760 | 759 | 758 | 757 | 756 | **755** |

8.

| 94 | **93** | 92 | 91 | 90 | 89 | 88 | **87** | 86 | 85 |

9.

| 723 | 722 | 721 | 720 | 719 | **718** | 717 | 716 | **715** | 714 |

10.

| 274 | 273 | **272** | 271 | 270 | 269 | **268** | 267 | 266 | 265 |

11.

| 388 | 387 | 386 | 385 | 384 | 383 | 382 | 381 | 380 | 379 |

12.

| 255 | 254 | 253 | 252 | 251 | 250 | 249 | 248 | 247 | 246 |

13.

| 48 | 47 | 46 | 45 | 44 | 43 | 42 | 41 | 40 | 39 |

14.

| 449 | 448 | 447 | 446 | 445 | 444 | 443 | 442 | 441 | 440 |

15.

| 39 | 38 | 37 | 36 | 35 | 34 | 33 | 32 | 31 | 30 |

16.

| 855 | 854 | 853 | 852 | 851 | 850 | 849 | 848 | 847 | 846 |

17.

| 318 | 317 | 316 | 315 | 314 | 313 | 312 | 311 | 310 | 309 |

18.

| 466 | 465 | 464 | 463 | 462 | 461 | 460 | 459 | 458 | 457 |

19.

| 12 | 11 | 10 | 9 | 8 | 7 | 6 | 5 | 4 | 3 |

20.

| 160 | 159 | 158 | 157 | 156 | 155 | 154 | 153 | 152 | 151 |

21.

| 313 | 312 | 311 | 310 | 309 | 308 | 307 | 306 | 305 | 304 |

22.

| 149 | **148** | **147** | 146 | 145 | 144 | 143 | 142 | 141 | 140 |

23.

| **293** | 292 | 291 | 290 | 289 | 288 | **287** | 286 | 285 | 284 |

24.

| 624 | 623 | 622 | **621** | **620** | 619 | 618 | 617 | 616 | 615 |

25.

| 872 | **871** | 870 | **869** | 868 | 867 | 866 | 865 | 864 | 863 |

26.

| 668 | **667** | 666 | **665** | 664 | 663 | 662 | 661 | 660 | 659 |

27.

| 300 | 299 | 298 | 297 | 296 | **295** | 294 | 293 | **292** | 291 |

28.

| **678** | 677 | 676 | 675 | 674 | **673** | 672 | 671 | 670 | 669 |

29.

| 885 | 884 | 883 | 882 | 881 | 880 | 879 | **878** | 877 | **876** |

30.

| 356 | **355** | 354 | 353 | 352 | 351 | **350** | 349 | 348 | 347 |

31.

| **43** | 42 | 41 | 40 | 39 | 38 | 37 | 36 | 35 | **34** |

32.

| 540 | 539 | 538 | 537 | 536 | 535 | **534** | 533 | 532 | **531** |

33.

412	**411**	410	409	408	407	406	**405**	404	403

34.

222	221	220	219	218	217	**216**	215	214	213

35.

54	53	52	51	50	**49**	48	47	**46**	45

36.

578	**577**	576	575	574	**573**	572	571	570	569

37.

31	30	29	28	**27**	26	25	24	23	22

38.

596	595	594	593	592	591	**590**	589	**588**	587

39.

42	41	40	39	**38**	37	**36**	35	34	33

40.

20	19	18	17	16	**15**	14	**13**	12	11

41.

52	**51**	50	49	48	**47**	46	45	44	43

42.

912	911	910	909	908	907	906	**905**	**904**	903

43.

761	760	759	758	757	**756**	**755**	754	753	752

44.

| 848 | 847 | 846 | 845 | **844** | 843 | 842 | **841** | 840 | 839 |

45.

| 788 | 787 | 786 | 785 | **784** | 783 | 782 | 781 | 780 | **779** |

46.

| **486** | 485 | 484 | 483 | **482** | 481 | 480 | 479 | 478 | 477 |

47.

| 530 | 529 | 528 | **527** | 526 | 525 | **524** | 523 | 522 | 521 |

48.

| 345 | 344 | 343 | 342 | 341 | 340 | **339** | 338 | 337 | **336** |

Page 8: Counting Down

49.

| 18 | **17** | **16** | 15 | 14 | 13 | 12 | 11 | 10 | 9 |

50.

| **267** | **266** | 265 | 264 | 263 | 262 | 261 | 260 | 259 | 258 |

51.

| 172 | 171 | 170 | 169 | **168** | **167** | 166 | 165 | 164 | 163 |

52.

| 326 | 325 | 324 | 323 | 322 | 321 | **320** | **319** | 318 | 317 |

53.

| 61 | 60 | 59 | 58 | 57 | **56** | **55** | 54 | 53 | 52 |

54.

| 923 | 922 | 921 | 920 | **919** | **918** | 917 | 916 | 915 | 914 |

55.

| 704 | 703 | 702 | **701** | **700** | 699 | 698 | 697 | 696 | 695 |

56.

| 340 | 339 | 338 | 337 | **336** | **335** | 334 | 333 | 332 | 331 |

57.

| 807 | **806** | **805** | 804 | 803 | 802 | 801 | 800 | 799 | 798 |

58.

| 708 | 707 | 706 | 705 | 704 | **703** | **702** | 701 | 700 | 699 |

59.

| 435 | 434 | 433 | 432 | 431 | 430 | **429** | **428** | 427 | 426 |

60.

| **504** | **503** | 502 | 501 | 500 | 499 | 498 | 497 | 496 | 495 |

61.

| 778 | **777** | **776** | 775 | 774 | 773 | 772 | 771 | 770 | 769 |

62.

| **537** | **536** | 535 | 534 | 533 | 532 | 531 | 530 | 529 | 528 |

63.

| 363 | 362 | 361 | 360 | 359 | 358 | 357 | **356** | **355** | 354 |

64.

| 279 | 278 | 277 | **276** | **275** | 274 | 273 | 272 | 271 | 270 |

65.

| 710 | 709 | 708 | **707** | **706** | 705 | 704 | 703 | 702 | 701 |

66.

| 609 | **608** | **607** | 606 | 605 | 604 | 603 | 602 | 601 | 600 |

67.

| 422 | **421** | **420** | 419 | 418 | 417 | 416 | 415 | 414 | 413 |

68.

| 813 | 812 | 811 | 810 | 809 | 808 | **807** | **806** | 805 | 804 |

69.

| 517 | 516 | **515** | **514** | 513 | 512 | 511 | 510 | 509 | 508 |

70.

| 914 | 913 | 912 | 911 | **910** | **909** | 908 | 907 | 906 | 905 |

71.

| 735 | 734 | 733 | 732 | 731 | 730 | 729 | **728** | **727** | 726 |

72.

| **718** | **717** | 716 | 715 | 714 | 713 | 712 | 711 | 710 | 709 |

73.

| 461 | 460 | 459 | 458 | 457 | **456** | **455** | 454 | 453 | 452 |

74.

| 257 | 256 | 255 | 254 | 253 | 252 | 251 | **250** | **249** | 248 |

75.

| 595 | 594 | 593 | 592 | 591 | **590** | **589** | 588 | 587 | 586 |

76.

| **500** | **499** | 498 | 497 | 496 | 495 | 494 | 493 | 492 | 491 |

77. | 256 | 255 | 254 | 253 | 252 | 251 | 250 | **249** | **248** | 247 |

78. | 328 | 327 | 326 | 325 | **324** | **323** | 322 | 321 | 320 | 319 |

79. | 574 | 573 | 572 | 571 | 570 | 569 | **568** | **567** | 566 | 565 |

80. | 394 | 393 | 392 | 391 | 390 | 389 | 388 | **387** | **386** | 385 |

81. | 322 | 321 | 320 | **319** | **318** | 317 | 316 | 315 | 314 | 313 |

82. | 727 | 726 | 725 | 724 | **723** | **722** | 721 | 720 | 719 | 718 |

83. | **446** | **445** | 444 | 443 | 442 | 441 | 440 | 439 | 438 | 437 |

84. | 204 | 203 | 202 | 201 | 200 | 199 | 198 | **197** | **196** | 195 |

85. | 124 | **123** | **122** | 121 | 120 | 119 | 118 | 117 | 116 | 115 |

86. | 189 | 188 | 187 | 186 | 185 | **184** | **183** | 182 | 181 | 180 |

87. | **851** | **850** | 849 | 848 | 847 | 846 | 845 | 844 | 843 | 842 |

88. | 781 | 780 | 779 | 778 | **777** | **776** | 775 | 774 | 773 | 772 |

89. | 803 | 802 | 801 | **800** | **799** | 798 | 797 | 796 | 795 | 794 |

90. | 494 | 493 | **492** | **491** | 490 | 489 | 488 | 487 | 486 | 485 |

91. | 758 | **757** | **756** | 755 | 754 | 753 | 752 | 751 | 750 | 749 |

92. | 897 | **896** | **895** | 894 | 893 | 892 | 891 | 890 | 889 | 888 |

93. | 749 | 748 | 747 | **746** | **745** | 744 | 743 | 742 | 741 | 740 |

94. | 550 | 549 | 548 | 547 | 546 | **545** | **544** | 543 | 542 | 541 |

95. | 407 | 406 | 405 | **404** | **403** | 402 | 401 | 400 | 399 | 398 |

96. | 17 | 16 | 15 | 14 | **13** | **12** | 11 | 10 | 9 | 8 |

Page 15: Counting Patterns

97. | **746** | 750 | 754 | 758 | 762 | 766 | 770 | 774 | 778 | 782 |

98. | 837 | 841 | 845 | 849 | 853 | 857 | 861 | 865 | **869** | 873 |

99.

| 194 | 197 | 200 | **203** | 206 | 209 | 212 | 215 | 218 | 221 |

100.

| 786 | 790 | **794** | 798 | 802 | 806 | 810 | 814 | 818 | 822 |

101.

| 32 | 36 | 40 | **44** | 48 | 52 | 56 | 60 | 64 | 68 |

102.

| 242 | 246 | 250 | 254 | 258 | 262 | 266 | 270 | 274 | **278** |

103.

| 34 | 36 | 38 | 40 | 42 | 44 | 46 | **48** | 50 | 52 |

104.

| 219 | 223 | 227 | 231 | 235 | 239 | 243 | **247** | 251 | 255 |

105.

| 461 | 464 | **467** | 470 | 473 | 476 | 479 | 482 | 485 | 488 |

106.

| 870 | 872 | **874** | 876 | 878 | 880 | 882 | 884 | 886 | 888 |

107.

| 762 | 766 | 770 | 774 | 778 | 782 | 786 | 790 | **794** | 798 |

108.

| 941 | 945 | **949** | 953 | 957 | 961 | 965 | 969 | 973 | 977 |

109.

| 482 | 486 | 490 | 494 | 498 | 502 | 506 | **510** | 514 | 518 |

110. | 479 | 482 | 485 | 488 | 491 | 494 | 497 | **500** | 503 | 506 |

111. | 832 | 835 | 838 | 841 | 844 | **847** | 850 | 853 | 856 | 859 |

112. | 457 | **461** | 465 | 469 | 473 | 477 | 481 | 485 | 489 | 493 |

113. | 456 | 461 | 466 | 471 | 476 | **481** | 486 | 491 | 496 | 501 |

114. | 302 | 305 | 308 | 311 | 314 | 317 | 320 | 323 | 326 | **329** |

115. | **687** | 691 | 695 | 699 | 703 | 707 | 711 | 715 | 719 | 723 |

116. | 480 | 482 | **484** | 486 | 488 | 490 | 492 | 494 | 496 | 498 |

117. | 751 | 754 | 757 | 760 | 763 | 766 | 769 | 772 | **775** | 778 |

118. | 365 | 367 | 369 | 371 | 373 | 375 | 377 | 379 | 381 | **383** |

119. | 765 | 768 | 771 | 774 | 777 | **780** | 783 | 786 | 789 | 792 |

120. | 418 | **421** | 424 | 427 | 430 | 433 | 436 | 439 | 442 | 445 |

121. 982	**985**	988	991	994	997	1,000	1,003	1,006	1,009
122. **643**	648	653	658	663	668	673	678	683	688
123. 736	740	**744**	748	752	756	760	764	768	772
124. **846**	849	852	855	858	861	864	867	870	873
125. 674	676	**678**	680	682	684	686	688	690	692
126. 905	908	911	**914**	917	920	923	926	929	932
127. 152	157	162	167	172	177	**182**	187	192	197
128. 893	**897**	901	905	909	913	917	921	925	929
129. 177	180	**183**	186	189	192	195	198	201	204
130. 547	550	553	556	559	562	565	568	**571**	574
131. 321	326	**331**	336	341	346	351	356	361	366

132.

| 713 | 717 | **721** | 725 | 729 | 733 | 737 | 741 | 745 | 749 |

133.

| 575 | 578 | 581 | 584 | 587 | 590 | 593 | 596 | **599** | 602 |

134.

| 945 | 948 | 951 | 954 | 957 | **960** | 963 | 966 | 969 | 972 |

135.

| 252 | 256 | 260 | 264 | 268 | 272 | 276 | **280** | 284 | 288 |

136.

| 730 | 733 | 736 | **739** | 742 | 745 | 748 | 751 | 754 | 757 |

137.

| 835 | 837 | 839 | 841 | **843** | 845 | 847 | 849 | 851 | 853 |

138.

| 273 | 275 | **277** | 279 | 281 | 283 | 285 | 287 | 289 | 291 |

139.

| **910** | 915 | 920 | 925 | 930 | 935 | 940 | 945 | 950 | 955 |

140.

| 38 | 43 | **48** | 53 | 58 | 63 | 68 | 73 | 78 | 83 |

141.

| 401 | 403 | 405 | 407 | 409 | 411 | 413 | 415 | 417 | **419** |

142.

| 929 | 931 | 933 | **935** | 937 | 939 | 941 | 943 | 945 | 947 |

143.

| 173 | 176 | 179 | 182 | 185 | 188 | 191 | **194** | 197 | 200 |

144.

| 313 | 317 | 321 | 325 | 329 | **333** | 337 | 341 | 345 | 349 |

145.

| 239 | 241 | 243 | 245 | 247 | **249** | 251 | 253 | 255 | 257 |

Page 25: Compare the Numbers

146. <   147. <   148. >   149. <   150. >   151. <   152. <   153. >

154. >   155. >   156. <   157. >   158. >   159. <   160. >   161. <

162. >   163. >   164. <   165. <   166. <   167. >   168. >   169. >

170. <   171. <   172. >   173. >   174. >   175. <   176. >   177. >

178. <   179. >   180. <   181. >   182. <   183. <   184. <   185. <

186. >   187. >   188. <   189. <   190. >   191. <   192. <   193. <

194. <   195. >   196. >   197. >   198. >   199. <   200. <   201. >

202. >   203. <   204. >   205. <   206. <   207. <

Page 29: Circle the Numbers

208. (553) 277 (76) 484 404

209. 911 791 744 (69)(997)

210. (211)(724) 271 301 581

211. (78) 418 656 245 (867)

212. 169 512 (873) 103 (74)

213. 504 (66) 597 957 (999)

214. 687 302 390 (250)(904)

215. 273 436 (90) 104 (609)

216. 439 (83) 697 164 (954)   217. 383 523 (55) (546) 165

218. 717 (728) 289 (126) 182   219. (41) 404 (972) 411 899

220. (846) 194 787 (69) 310   221. (909) 335 (21) 396 308

222. (641) (328) 552 636 428   223. (87) (814) 709 149 690

224. (980) (11) 52 792 283   225. (959) (13) 265 69 863

226. (869) 464 679 (204) 763   227. 245 295 628 (854) (45)

228. (49) 503 (659) 239 524   229. 389 177 652 (697) (95)

230. (227) 694 824 720 (919)   231. 835 (143) (995) 786 351

232. 896 (71) (951) 532 438   233. (178) 649 348 (873) 184

234. 791 187 (855) (105) 642   235. 478 352 812 (269) (893)

236. 783 (361) 568 (973) 637   237. (175) 640 (958) 285 927

238. (103) 300 (842) 503 148   239. (977) 551 (127) 800 346

240. 740 (828) 778 513 (304)   241. (40) (839) 719 78 441

242. 484 (330) 726 (892) 568   243. 536 503 (978) 895 (264)

244. 538 690 (63) (946) 82   245. 491 (345) 352 (956) 665

246. (926) 226 (13) 922 154   247. (954) 582 (55) 670 597

248. (336) (920) 881 844 444

249. 772 (573) (949) 935 612

250. 475 573 (232) 536 (808)

251. (50) 765 (832) 432 812

252. 695 487 (763) (413) 514

253. (258) 317 (804) 739 613

254. (953) 448 308 (298) 928

255. 618 (809) (219) 502 309

256. (917) 395 417 345 (190)

257. 354 (994) 476 115 (104)

258. (190) 749 622 857 (902)

259. (848) (157) 468 330 186

260. 455 (769) (210) 323 658

261. (27) 265 (934) 608 191

262. 241 546 331 (123) (895)

263. 300 (71) (419) 223 161

264. (264) (840) 690 636 423

265. 204 (825) 451 395 (80)

266. 461 341 (889) (316) 854

267. 148 186 (94) (686) 164

268. 89 (61) 868 (923) 863

269. 643 (419) 500 (961) 602

270. 777 738 246 (170) (922)

271. 614 (80) 574 (899) 454

272. (201) (813) 539 528 729

273. (899) 657 (15) 269 747

274. 115 (977) 733 (59) 72

275. (204) (972) 766 772 780

276. 784 326 490 (793) (302)

277. (723) (95) 720 394 240

Page 34: Missing Numbers

278. 69 71   279. 195   280. 962   281. 521

282. 196   283. 985   284. 232   285. 489

286. 7   287. 98 100   288. 642   289. 802

290. 671   291. 324 326   292. 227   293. 805

294. 621   295. 679 681   296. 783 785   297. 98

298. 682 684   299. 573   300. 794   301. 96

302. 305 307   303. 718   304. 622 624   305. 599

306. 812   307. 563   308. 952   309. 116

310. 160   311. 786   312. 537   313. 17 19

314. 91   315. 37   316. 743   317. 325

318. 780   319. 441 443   320. 290   321. 316

322. 432   323. 691 693   324. 940   325. 846

326. 518   327. 650 652   328. 595   329. 739

330. 486   331. 817   332. 640 642   333. 13

334. 749   335. 310   336. 335   337. 898

338. 733   339. 770 772   340. 294   341. 565

342. 456   343. 492   344. 342 344   345. 698

346. 311   347. 241

Page 38: Ordering Numbers

348.	512	164	349.	468	186	350.	393	393	351.	748	339
	430	430		376	376		953	587		602	602
	164	479		520	468		645	645		644	644
	479	512		186	520		587	953		339	748

352. 341 117
155 155
117 341
655 655

353. 737 342
841 504
504 737
342 841

354. 559 216
856 559
216 595
595 856

355. 421 174
989 421
522 522
174 989

356. 668 167
167 210
210 444
444 668

357. 548 361
506 506
583 548
361 583

358. 544 414
475 475
636 544
414 636

359. 457 123
412 412
509 457
123 509

360. 626 277
871 588
277 626
588 871

361. 536 149
836 536
149 607
607 836

362. 758 179
179 191
569 569
191 758

363. 274 274
944 673
673 944
969 969

364. 330 243
358 330
243 358
783 783

365. 183 183
320 320
802 536
536 802

366. 108 108
580 297
498 498
297 580

367. 796 134
889 622
622 796
134 889

368. 712 456
456 712
975 763
763 975

369. 464 464
906 544
544 744
744 906

370. 512 217
739 512
539 539
217 739

371. 368 368
728 494
494 535
535 728

372. 316 134
134 316
613 613
986 986

373. 277 277
681 371
371 571
571 681

374. 385 385
421 421
638 638
821 821

375. 873 382
382 479
479 873
984 984

376. 277 157
775 277
157 652
652 775

377. 369 141
141 369
380 380
651 651

378. 168 168
495 187
187 495
808 808

379. 677 275
843 677
989 843
275 989

380.	782	635	381.	190	190	382.	985	348	383.	540	540
	635	782		200	200		348	509		976	877
	973	870		718	718		509	846		961	961
	870	973		923	923		846	985		877	976
384.	236	236	385.	889	334	386.	130	130	387.	642	153
	400	318		334	830		393	304		802	287
	719	400		830	888		304	393		287	642
	318	719		888	889		462	462		153	802
388.	268	268	389.	820	340	390.	701	212	391.	482	166
	423	423		985	759		882	701		915	482
	457	457		340	820		212	882		754	754
	878	878		759	985		955	955		166	915
392.	856	370	393.	692	143	394.	738	738	395.	813	813
	370	407		143	147		789	789		943	841
	829	829		147	692		907	859		841	943
	407	856		940	940		859	907		952	952
396.	904	171	397.	248	248	398.	726	148	399.	898	149
	993	497		280	280		148	220		593	236
	171	904		348	348		220	444		149	593
	497	993		977	977		444	726		236	898
400.	776	353	401.	911	353	402.	538	174	403.	862	298
	937	400		974	904		174	182		298	431
	400	776		353	911		802	538		431	492
	353	937		904	974		182	802		492	862
404.	511	170	405.	690	563	406.	319	319	407.	966	693
	794	511		668	668		893	377		693	743
	170	515		563	690		704	704		817	817
	515	794		697	697		377	893		743	966

408. 274 274
     927 405
     443 443
     405 927

409. 652 138
     345 345
     138 639
     639 652

410. 699 261
     261 643
     657 657
     643 699

411. 982 574
     867 867
     885 885
     574 982

412. 342 342
     511 511
     656 656
     752 752

413. 644 469
     469 524
     524 644
     875 875

414. 269 269
     481 481
     688 488
     488 688

415. 584 451
     451 530
     764 584
     530 764

416. 444 397
     629 444
     923 629
     397 923

417. 157 157
     336 161
     161 215
     215 336

418. 199 199
     807 343
     343 680
     680 807

419. 762 371
     371 691
     691 762
     954 954

420. 282 263
     820 282
     263 802
     802 820

421. 317 269
     573 317
     269 323
     323 573

422. 630 203
     203 447
     454 454
     447 630

423. 713 298
     588 358
     358 588
     298 713

424. 408 408
     409 409
     650 650
     738 738

425. 238 107
     107 238
     727 656
     656 727

426. 759 189
     810 759
     189 810
     944 944

427. 466 220
     220 266
     266 335
     335 466

428. 166 166
     837 536
     536 694
     694 837

429. 453 147
     895 453
     961 895
     147 961

430. 112 112
     492 132
     660 492
     132 660

431. 511 163
     612 511
     163 612
     769 769

432. 566 465
     541 541
     667 566
     465 667

433. 393 195
     365 365
     503 393
     195 503

434. 467 192
     192 467
     962 810
     810 962

435. 570 570
     872 743
     956 872
     743 956

436.	342	146	437.	366	156	438.	853	157	439.	624	171
	146	342		249	169		157	255		270	270
	679	482		156	249		497	497		171	624
	482	679		169	366		255	853		822	822
440.	187	187	441.	920	529	442.	638	420	443.	520	265
	492	492		529	791		656	638		862	284
	865	801		849	849		420	656		284	520
	801	865		791	920		761	761		265	862